TWIGS AND BONE

Tiffany Antone

BROADWAY PLAY PUBLISHING INC
New York
www.broadwayplaypublishing.com
info@broadwayplaypublishing.com

Cover art by DALL-E

First edition: July 2023
I S B N: 978-0-88145-987-6

Book design: Marie Donovan
Page make-up: Adobe InDesign
Typeface: Palatino

TWIGS AND BONE premiered with Nu Sass
Productions in Washington, DC, running from 1
April-25 June 2022. The cast and creative contributors
were:

MOIRA...Aubri O'Connor
BONNIE .... Lynn Sharp Spears
WILLIAM.. Tom Howley

Director/Props .... Lynn Sharp Spears
Assistant Director/Fights & Choreography ..Mundy Spears
Set ....Simone Schneeberg, Dan Remmers
Lights ....Helen Garcia-Alton
Sound .... Charles Lasky & Mik Bear
Costumes..Stephenie Yee
Stage Manager ....Charles Lasky
Assistant Stage Manager.............................Laurel Lehman
Marketing images ....Mik Bear
Advertising ....Laolu Fayese

The play received additional developmental support
from Hawthornden Writer's Retreat, Great Plains
Theatre Conference, and Acadiana Repertory Theatre.

CHARACTERS & SETTING

Bonnie Lane, 62, *a storm unto herself*

William Lane, 66, *a man who has misplaced his life*

Moira Lane, 30, *their daughter who grew up in this house, a woman who's made great pains to distance herself from the past*

Time: *August, unrooted*

Place: *A house that lives way off the beaten track in a gully all its own*

ABOUT THE DIALOGUE

The use of "—" in dialogue marks an interruption, whereas speeches with a "/" indicate an overlap in dialogue.

Additionally, there are several places in the script where beats are marked by character's names. These beats are moments of primal recognition, silent communication, pissing contests, impossible pain, and (sometimes) epiphany. In other words, these beats are felt/thought by the characters and need last only as long as the moment/feeling/thought requires.

And finally, although they've been living in the states (and in this house) for nigh on thirty years, BONNIE and WILLIAM are both of Irish origin. This does not mean they must speak with a full Irish dialect, but Ireland is definitely in charge of their rhythm.

ABOUT THE SPECTACLE

TWIGS AND BONE is a wild play, filled with spectacle
that has been intentionally rendered in poetic speak
rather than architectural schema. That's because I want
each production team to have fun determining how
to make the show work with their unique space and
resources. BUT, I also understand that some of the
stage directions in this play might take your breath
away, which is why I've included a list of maybes
and cheat codes at the end of the play to help get you
breathing again.

ACT ONE

Scene 1

(The stage presents a dank, dark, house that rarely sees sunlight except on the rare occasion when a well-intentioned soul cracks a window. A porch overlooks the dusty road out front and may sport a swing. A neglected screen door allows entrance.)

(Inside, the furniture is well used, especially the sofa which always remembers where its most favored occupants regularly sit. Various coffee cups reside in odd places...near windows, the door and some other dark places. There could be some plants, if they are accustomed to being ignored and allowed to run wild. And books...there should be lots of books. The occasional baby toy, brightly out of place, keeps the dank company.)

(MOIRA LANE, a rather regular looking woman of about 30, is currently struggling up the porch-steps of a memory she desperately avoids. Her suitcase, as if sensing her dread, lags behind.)

(She glares at a useless cell phone, rendered dumb by the isolated nature of their surroundings.)

MOIRA: Goddamn, middle of nowhere... *(She takes a breath. It's not the phone's fault... It's only a few days...)* Shit. *(She manages a very restrained knock... followed by a second, more decisive, knock.)*

(The quiet suffocates, as does the heat. MOIRA *mops her brow.)*

(Knock, knock, knock)

(Someone inside mutters and shuffles.)

*(*WILLIAM LANE, *a man who has misplaced his life, opens the door.)*

WILLIAM: You've made it.

MOIRA: Yes, unhappily so. I don't suppose you've got the air conditioner on in there?

WILLIAM: Of course. Of course. Let me just get my things.

MOIRA: What?

WILLIAM: You've come to take me away, right? You got my letters? My phone calls?

MOIRA: No, dad, I'm here for a visit—

WILLIAM: You can't stay. You can't stay! I sent letters, where are my, surely you got the…you want to come in and *visit*?

MOIRA: Yes, dad, I've brought a suitcase. A small suitcase—

WILLIAM: No, no, no. Let me get my things. She's upstairs, she won't even know I've gone—

MOIRA: Don't be ridiculous—Mom!

*(*WILLIAM *puts his hand to his ears, shuffles away.)*

(The screen door, unaccustomed to visitors, slaps MOIRA *in the face.)*

WILLIAM: Pure stubborn, hardheadedness…

MOIRA: Have you gone mad? *(She wrestles the door open and steps inside. The suitcase does not want to follow.)* I could use some help—

(WILLIAM *walks to the couch where he sits, hands to ears,
and humming.*)

MOIRA: Jesus Christ. Mom! Hello?

WILLIAM: Well don't go calling her in here. She's going
to get all uppity with you hollering like that.

(*The suitcase finally acquiesces and slides miserably inside.*)

(MOIRA *looks around.*)

MOIRA: It smells strange in here.

WILLIAM: Earthen.

MOIRA: What? No. (*Sniffs*) Like mold. You should
open some windows or something. Isn't that woman
cleaning?

WILLIAM: Who?

MOIRA: Fleur.

WILLIAM: Fleur's gone. Fleur di'lis vanishimo.

MOIRA: She's, what? I don't understand—ow. (*She steps
on a squeaky toy.*) Did you get a dog?

WILLIAM: I hate dogs, you know that.

(*Squeak*)

(WILLIAM *turns to look.*)

WILLIAM: (*Chuckles*) Oh. That.

(MOIRA *waits for an explanation, but none comes. She
clenches down hard on her irritation.*)

MOIRA: MOM!

(*A voice from upstairs floats down with matched
aggravation.*)

BONNIE: (*OS*) What in hell you yelling for? (*A rather
clumsy collection of aggravated thumps precede her arrival.
Descending the stairs:*) Sounds like a pack of animals

down here, all that shouting! What on earth could be so important? *(She enters, a force of nature misguided.)*

MOIRA: Uh, me?

BONNIE: Twiggy! My God, I should have known. That voice, always so shrill. You are your father's daughter, right? Shouting away like that. Didn't you tell her to be quiet?

WILLIAM: —I told her—

BONNIE: Didn't he tell you to be quiet?

MOIRA: Yes, he told me to be quiet, but I don't really understand—

BONNIE: Never listen, just like your father.

(WILLIAM snorts.)

BONNIE: It's true. Why when I think how much time I've wasted just talking at the two of you, never sinking in— "Stop yelling, don't run in the house, don't cut your hair…" I've got another life in there somewhere, another life's worth of living just wasted on handing out advice.

(MOIRA)

(WILLIAM)

(MOIRA)

MOIRA: Why's the phone disconnected?

BONNIE: Is that why you're here?

MOIRA: I haven't heard from Fleur in weeks. I've been trying to call—

BONNIE: I got tired of it ringing.

MOIRA: Well, are you alright?

BONNIE: You can see I'm alright. I'm standing here looking at you, ain't I? Jesus, will you get a load of this one Willy?

(WILLIAM *disappears into a book.*)

MOIRA: I was worried.

BONNIE: Ach.

MOIRA: /Where's Fleur?

BONNIE: /Worried she says.

MOIRA: I'm not— What?

BONNIE: Come out here to fuss. Like we was a couple of babes?

MOIRA: *Where* is *Fleur*?

BONNIE: The pollinator? Harbinger of dust, dander, and other things that make your nose itch? The girl was a disaster, dear. Never hire a maid named after vegetation.

MOIRA: I've paid her through September!

BONNIE: Well, then I'm afraid you've been taken. She left out of here around, what would you say William, July? The night of the fireworks. When was that?

MOIRA: The *4th of July*?

BONNIE: Ach, no, what do you think I've gone completely bonkers? There was the 4th, of course, and then there was some sort of local thing after. Right about the 18th or something, a grand opening I think it was. I'll never forget it. She flew out that door, silhouetted with a spray of hot pink and blue behind her. I thought to myself, "That girl can't clean a lick, but God, what an exit!"

MOIRA: You let her go last month?

BONNIE: What "Let go", the poor girl took off running. I didn't like her much, but I'd never send her off in the late of night like that. She quit.

(MOIRA *looks for someone, anyone, to share in her disbelief.* WILLIAM *is not that someone.*)

MOIRA: Mom!

BONNIE: What?

MOIRA: That's the *eighth* woman I've hired—

BONNIE: Are you going to be staying for long, because your voice is really starting to needle my nerves—

MOIRA: Why'd she go running?

BONNIE: Oh, who knows, she's French. They've never made a lot of sense to me.

MOIRA: Do you understand how difficult it is to find a good live-in? They're practically impossible these days, and forget French. She was practically a goddamned national treasure! You must have done something—

WILLIAM: Said it wasn't in her job description.

BONNIE: Oh, now that was a/ load of—

MOIRA: /*What* wasn't in her job description?

WILLIAM: Changing, burping, cleaning up its shit—

BONNIE: I object to that, I object very strongly to that. I have been doing the lion's share, I just ask for a little assistance now and then—

(WILLIAM *snorts.*)

BONNIE: And what would you know about it, anyway? Down here all day, bibbling the scotch like a right 'aul rummy.

MOIRA: Can you two just, stop, for one goddamn second?

(*Silence*)

(BONNIE *huffs.*)

BONNIE: I see no need for that kind of language.

MOIRA: Five minutes in this house and my head already feels like exploding. (*Breath*) Okay, one of you, and I don't care who, please just tell me what is going on.

WILLIAM: Your mother's gone and had herself another baby. And I take an occasional drink in the afternoon to forget what an auld whore she's become.

BONNIE: Occasional my ass—

MOIRA: Wait, a what?

WILLIAM: The girl said looking after little ones wasn't in her job description and she lit off for the train. I think she called a cab first—

BONNIE: Well, really, what sort of maid did you ever hear of that didn't know how to wash nappies? It's not like I was asking her to wet nurse.

MOIRA: I don't think I heard you right—

WILLIAM: If she didn't agree to it, and didn't want to do it, you shouldn't have tried to make her do it. You can't force someone to do something they didn't agree to do, now can you?

BONNIE: Oof, what a lot of rubbish.

WILLIAM: Bah.

MOIRA: What *baby*?

BONNIE: Maeb.

(MOIRA *is frozen.*)

MOIRA: Say that name again?

BONNIE: Ach, no, you heard it the first time, I can tell by the grimace spread cross your cheeks. Course, you won't understand, haven't heard mention of your sister's name out your lips since she passed. And why is that? Hoarding all that grief, are you? Is that it? Think you have license to it all by yourself? Well I was her mother you know! The name don't belong to the child, it belongs to the parent.

(MOIRA*)*

(MOIRA)

(BONNIE *adjusts her hair.)*

BONNIE: Well, say something.

MOIRA: I don't understand…how, you would—

WILLIAM: What's to understand? She went out last Autumn, had herself an affair, and got herself knocked up—

BONNIE: Now, William—

WILLIAM: Only way I can see it! I haven't touched you in years, always barking at me about one thing or another, never about that. I gave up. Had I known she had an itch, I could've scratched. As it is now, I won't touch her, she's gone and spoilt the well—

(MORIA and her hollow stomach.)

MOIRA: I need to sit down…

WILLIAM: Don't never drink from a spoilt well Moira. No matter how thirsty you may be.

MOIRA: But you're sixty-five years old…

BONNIE: Sixty-two, you damn ingrate. *(To* WILLIAM*)* And don't go insulting my honor. It was a miraculous conception, I told you that!

(WILLIAM makes raspberry sounds.)

MOIRA: *(No one is listening)* A…baby. And you named her after…but that's not possible—

WILLIAM: You're about as miraculous as 'aul Gurny Smith down there on the corner, liftin' her skirts for a Franklin!

BONNIE: Now, don't you start insultin' me!

WILLIAM: I'll insult you all I want, traipsin' your rotten 'aul snatch around this place like we was supposed

to bend down and pray to it. I'll not buy into that
propaganda, no matter how far beneath the earth you
may have buried my balls!

MOIRA: WILL YOU BOTH PLEASE SHUT UP! /God,
my head!

(BONNIE's *ears prick up.*)

BONNIE: /Jesus, Mary and Joseph, now look what
you've done.

MOIRA: Where are you going?

(WILLIAM *throws his hands down in disgust.*)

BONNIE: Upstairs. You've waken up little Maeb. You
with that shrill voice of yours, just like your father,
peck, peck, peckin' at me all the time. *(She heads up the
stairs.)* Poor thing, crying her eyes out because of you.
Nice introduction, wouldn't you say? Encountering
you in one of your moods.

MOIRA: I don't hear anything.

BONNIE: Well how could you, yelling like that.

(MOIRA *steps after* BONNIE.)

BONNIE: And just where do you think you're going?

MOIRA: To see this *baby*—

BONNIE: I don't think so! Coming in from God knows
where, with God knows what kind of germs on ya'—
We're all over used to one another here. You're a—
what do they call 'em Willy? —Foreign germs, you've
got. You're practically toxic, by comparison.

MOIRA: I'm not *toxic*—

BONNIE: Ha! William, help Twiggy with her suitcase,
and fetch her a cab for Godsakes.

MOIRA: You think I'm *leaving*?

BONNIE: Why not? You've just come to make sure we was alright, haven't you? Well we're fine. Go on and get out of here before you stir things up to a boil.

MOIRA: I'm not stirring—

BONNIE: William! Get off your soggy ass and contribute! *(She disappears up the stairs.)*

(WILLIAM looks up at MOIRA.)

WILLIAM: So you want a yellow cab then, or should I just loan you her broom?

(Lights fade.)

Scene 2

(MOIRA scrubs away at the kitchen—the sink, the cupboards, the floor. It could all use a good cleaning.)

(Her suitcase keeps nervous watch from the corner.)

(WILLIAM comes in for a snack. He carries his book. He looks at MOIRA. It takes him a while to work up the right words.)

(They don't come.)

WILLIAM: Won't make no difference, you know.

MOIRA: What?

WILLIAM: Scrubbing away like that. Comes right back.

(MOIRA and the dirt.)

MOIRA: How long has she been like that?

WILLIAM: Like what?

MOIRA: A baby? Really dad? And why would she call it that?

WILLIAM: I dunno, said the woods told her it was your sister reincarnated or something.

MOIRA: Jesus!

WILLIAM: If you ask me, she's just trying to soften me up a bit so I won't be mad about the affair. Can't admit she got caught. Just turns up with a baby one day. "It's a miracle!" She'd been looking a little fat, I thought she'd just been eating too much. That Fleur used a lot of butter. Never ate so much cheese in my entire life. You know I'm supposed to be on a low cholesterol diet—

MOIRA: Did she steal it?

WILLIAM: No, it stayed right there, cloggin' up my arteries.

MOIRA: The baby, dad.

WILLIAM: Oh, no, no looks like her plain enough. And like I said, she'd been getting fat. Had an ass on her, you know. Course, I suppose I couldn't say for sure. She's always dressed. Gets up dressed, goes to sleep dressed, comes out of the shower dressed. Hell, I don't think I've seen that woman without her clothes on since 1983.

MOIRA: Well she's obviously…I mean, you don't just go having babies at her age, affair or— And she has the audacity to claim that it's, it's…she doesn't believe in reincarnation!

WILLIAM: What are you doing down there? Didn't you hear me tell you it don't matter?

MOIRA: Three days. Three days I take off work, to come here, to sort this place out, to sort you both out—I'm going to spend the whole time on my hands and knees. Wasn't Fleur cleaning?

WILLIAM: Hell yes, she was cleaning. Cleaning day and night, woman never stopped cleaning, only time she stopped cleaning was to cook up some butter and cheese. Put it on a plate. Make me eat it. You ever have crepes?

MOIRA: Yes.

WILLIAM: Damn good, those are. Wish your mother hadn't scared her off like that. You want a sandwich? *(He rustles in the fridge.)*

MOIRA: No thanks.

WILLIAM: Suit yourself.

(MOIRA and the floor.)

MOIRA: She was supposed to be cleaning. And preparing low-cholesterol meals for you. And keeping an eye on things. She never told me about…any of this.

WILLIAM: I did. I wrote up and down, every day, miles of letters screaming "Help, get me outta' here. I can't sleep"

MOIRA: I never got any.

WILLIAM: Really? Huh. Maybe I just dreamt them then. *(He takes a bite into his sandwich. It's dry as dust. He applies more mayonnaise.)*

MOIRA: Where do you keep the car keys?

WILLIAM: What, to the Mercedes? Your mother turned it into a flower pot.

MOIRA: She *what*?

WILLIAM: Full of dirt. She planted marigolds or daisi-golds, or some such fool sort of thing in there.

MOIRA: How can a sixty two year old woman flood a car with mud and plants and you don't say anything about it?

WILLIAM: Didn't notice / 'till I tried to take it out for a drive—

MOIRA: /Didn't notice?!

WILLIAM: What are you still doing down there? I told you to get up off of that floor already! Not fit to go crawling around on the ground like a peasant, it don't come up!

(MOIRA *stops scrubbing.*)

MOIRA: If she turned the car into a garden, then how are you getting in to town? How are you getting your groceries for Godsakes?

WILLIAM: Delivery service.

MOIRA: Jesus Christ!

WILLIAM: No, just some pimply kid, probably saving up for college.

(MOIRA*'s frustration bubbles out of her on bed of vowels.*)

(BONNIE *joins* MOIRA *and* WILLIAM.)

BONNIE: Oh. You're still here.

MOIRA: Dad says you turned the car into a flower pot.

BONNIE: Ai, and it's a damn sight prettier that way. And more useful. Did your father tell you he wanted to drive it off the bridge? I saved his life, I did. Are you— What are you doing on the ground? You're not cleaning are you? Is she cleaning?

MOIRA: Yes.

(BONNIE *laughs.*)

WILLIAM: I told her.

MOIRA: Told me what?

(BONNIE *takes a bottle from the cupboard, proceeds to fill it and heat it, without missing a beat.*)

BONNIE: What do you want with the car anyway?

MOIRA: I thought I'd go into town and see if anyone had reported a missing baby.

BONNIE: Oh, look who's feeling clever. Isn't that funny William? Twiggy thinks she's being clever.

MOIRA: Moira.

BONNIE: You have filled out a bit... Hasn't she filled out a bit? Used to be so damn skinny she could slide through walls—

(MOIRA *bites her tongue.*)

BONNIE: —Used to be certain she'd slip down a crack if she came across one in the sidewalk.

MOIRA: I didn't come all the way out here so you could bother me about my weight.

BONNIE: Look, *Moira*, it's not my fault you dragged yourself all the way out here, uninvited, like this. We're perfectly fine /so why don't you just call yourself a cab// and—

MOIRA: /Fine? You are not "Fine"// Because the phone's been disconnected.

BONNIE: So go out and stick your thumb up in the air. I'm sure someone will stop.

MOIRA: Mother—

BONNIE: Uh-oh, the dreaded two-syllable salute. I'm about to get it now—

MOIRA: Can you just stop for one second and listen to me?

BONNIE: Oh, Moira, I just hate the way your voice sounds when you get serious—

MOIRA: Oh my God! Look, things have obviously crawled way past "Ordinary" here, and I'm trying to figure out just how far. I mean, is there a "Wanted" poster out with your face on it? Are you claiming "Aliens did it"? / I know you don't have the kind of money it would take for fertility—

BONNIE: /I knew it! I knew you'd come swooping in, reading into things, and just shit all over it. William, you didn't put mayonnaise on that sandwich did you?

MOIRA: That's not what I'm doing!

BONNIE: Oh, no? / William?

MOIRA: /No.

WILLIAM: Of course I used mayonnaise, the bread's as dry as a bone.

BONNIE: You know you're not supposed to have that.

MOIRA: Hello, I'm talking here—

BONNIE: Do you know, Moira, that that flower head you hired was trying to kill your father? Down here everyday, "Would you like more sauce Monsieur Lane?" Just pouring it on! Murderess!

WILLIAM: She was a godsend!

BONNIE: Stop eating that.

MOIRA: Mom!

BONNIE: Moira, your father and I are trying to have a conversation.

WILLIAM: No, you're trying to tell me what to do!

BONNIE: Give me the sandwich.

WILLIAM: No.

BONNIE: Give me the goddamned sandwich Willy. Give it to me, give it to me now!

(BONNIE *reaches for the sandwich but* WILLIAM *shovels it, in its entirety, into his mouth.*)

MOIRA: Jesus Christ.

BONNIE: Animal!

(WILLIAM *growls and grins.*)

(*But then he starts to choke.*)

(MOIRA *jumps into action.*)

(BONNIE *tests the baby bottle.*)

MOIRA: Oh my God, Dad! Mom, call the—God damnit, the phone. Dad? Can you breathe?

(MOIRA *hits her father on the back until he spits the remains of his sandwich onto the table.*)

(WILLIAM *takes in a great breath.*)

BONNIE: Jesus Christ Moira, haven't you ever learnt the Heimlich maneuver? You're lucky you didn't kill him. (*She leaves with the bottle.*)

(MOIRA *looks at* WILLIAM.)

MOIRA: Are you okay?

(WILLIAM *looks at the sandwich, he picks it up.*)

WILLIAM: Will you look at that? I had no idea my mouth was so big.

(MOIRA *storms after* BONNIE *into the living room.*)

MOIRA: Don't walk away from me!

BONNIE: I'm not walking away from you dear, I'm walking towards Maeb.

MOIRA: Stop calling her that! Did you steal that baby?

BONNIE: Now how could you ask me such a thing?

(MOIRA *stares.* BONNIE *rolls her eyes.*)

BONNIE: Ach, no, I did not steal any baby.

MOIRA: Did you find it then?

BONNIE: I told you—

MOIRA: There's no such thing as miracles!

(BONNIE *slaps her face.* MOIRA *freezes.*)

BONNIE: Now you listen here Missy, I'll tolerate a lot of things out of you, but don't you come near me blaspheming the unknown.

MOIRA: You're *too old*.

BONNIE: Maybe, *maybe*, but fortunately for me and Maeb, it's not you who gets to make those kind of decisions.

(MOIRA. BONNIE. MOIRA)

MOIRA: I want to see her.

BONNIE: You want?

MOIRA: Yes.

BONNIE: *You. Want.*

MOIRA: Yes. I'm all cleaned up, no "foreign" germs left to speak of. If she really is, if you really had another baby, I should…meet her.

BONNIE: You think hiring some fancy French woman to come into our home and clean up the things you don't want to look at gives you privileges?

MOIRA: I—

BONNIE: I don't even know where you live. You hire someone, some strange *French* girl, and send her to us without even asking if we so much as want her, and I can't send her back because I don't even know your address. And now you show up, at *my* home, and start making demands of *me*? As if I owe you anything? I don't. So no. You can't see her. You haven't earned it.

(BONNIE *stomps upstairs,* MOIRA *stares.*)

(*After a moment* WILLIAM *enters, swallowing the last of his sandwich.*)

WILLIAM: Weather fit for fighting. Turn the goddamn light on, will ya?

MOIRA: She's crazy.

WILLIAM: Your mother's always been… complicated—

MOIRA: *Complicated*?

WILLIAM: Getting older just isn't the medicine they tell you it's going to be.

MOIRA: This is obviously going to take more time than I thought…

WILLIAM: Always been trouble between the two of you. I hoped you'd come back to some common ground once you'd gotten far enough away. Loop yourself back to the source so to speak. You're a lot alike you know.

MOIRA: What! How can you say that? We are *nothing*/ alike—

WILLIAM: /Then again, maybe that's why you pick at one another so well. Hard to look at yourself without passing judgement. Course, I never had the privilege of meeting my mirror, so I don't know. Imagine that's why your sister was so easy to be around—different from us all. Sweetest damn thing ever walked the planet. Sat in there with your mother, fits an all, never even batting an eye—

MOIRA: A prisoner.

WILLIAM: What?

MOIRA: Mom is an emotional vacuum. She sucked her dry. (*Barely*) You just weren't here enough to see it. And she wasn't—Maeb wasn't perfect. She was fragile. Too fragile for this family. God made a mistake giving her to us.

(WILLIAM *sucks his teeth, thinking. Walks to the screen door*)

WILLIAM: Hope you got a strong back. You'll have to sleep on the sofa tonight, not the nicest of nests.

MOIRA: What? I can't sleep on the— What's wrong with my old room?

WILLIAM: Ach, your mother's gone and turned it over to the baby. Threw my newspapers out without even a warning. Whole place is dedicated to little pink booties and lace. It's disgusting.

MOIRA: I don't believe it. I DON'T BELIEVE IT.

WILLIAM: Believing's got nothing to do with it. Will you turn on that light already? The sky's gone and swallowed the sun and I can't see where my body ends and the world begins.

(Black)

Scene 3

(It is late, the wind is restless.)

(MOIRA can't sleep. She wanders the living room, looking at old photos, knickknacks. She picks up a frame, is disgusted by the dirt beneath, and starts to wipe, only to realize it's a much bigger job than a simple swipe of her finger.)

(She picks up a coffee cup, looks inside, sniffs and quickly recoils.)

(WILLIAM shuffles downstairs.)

MOIRA: What is this?

WILLIAM: Ach, you scared the living daylights out of me. What are you doing scurrying around down there?

MOIRA: I can't sleep. What the hell is this?

(WILLIAM squints into the dark.)

WILLIAM: Can't see what you're asking about there—

MOIRA: It's a coffee cup full of, what smells like, urine. Please tell me it's not.

WILLIAM: Ach, don't go messing with that now!

MOIRA: Dad?

WILLIAM: You put it back where you found it. Down here nosing around where you don't belong. Put it back!

MOIRA: But—

WILLIAM: I got to have some sort of peace in my own home, don't I? Some sort of place to call my own?

MOIRA: Oh my God… So you're, what? Marking your territory?

WILLIAM: Don't expect you to understand. Put it back now. Interfering with things you can't possibly understand— And don't go messing about with your mother's frames either. One of them portraits goes out of place, your mother descends like an angry hawk.

(MOIRA *looks around. How can this mess claim any sort of order?*)

MOIRA: Jesus.

WILLIAM: *(Shouts to the ceiling)* Christ Almighty, will you shut her up already? *(To* MOIRA*)* Damn that child, she's crying my ear off.

MOIRA: I don't hear anything.

WILLIAM: Have you gone deaf? She's ready to shake the house to its foundations! Your mother fancies she got herself an ear infection or something. I came down for a hot toddy.

MOIRA: For the baby?

WILLIAM: No, for my nerves, ai, you don't give brandy to a baby. Jesus H Christ, good thing you haven't multiplied yet. You haven't have you?

MOIRA: No.

WILLIAM: Good. You might want to read a book or something before you do.

MOIRA: *(Muttering)* Yeah, I'll be sure to do that.

WILLIAM: You want a drink?

MOIRA: God, yes.

(MOIRA *looks around, the house is silent.*)

(WILLIAM *pours the brandy.*)

(MOIRA *senses a small but permanent tearing in the universe.*)

MOIRA: Dad, is the baby crying *now*?

WILLIAM: Look who wants to be funny.

MOIRA: I'm not trying to be—

WILLIAM: Of course she's crying. You think we got a pack of coyotes or something up there. Your mother's illegitimate spawn is RUINING MY BEAUTY SLEEP.

(BONNIE'*s angry footsteps tumble down the stairs.*)

BONNIE: What in the name of all that's holy are you thinking yelling like that?

(MOIRA *closes her eyes in search of sense.*)

WILLIAM: Me?

BONNIE: Yes, you, with your loudness, you're unbearable LOUDness.

WILLIAM: Oh, I'm sorry. Am I *disturbing* you?

BONNIE: Yes, you are.

WILLIAM: Well, good. You know what else is disturbing? Being woken up at all hours of the night by a shrieking baby when you're sixty six years old! For fuck's sake, didn't we do this already?

(MOIRA *looks around. The tear is getting bigger.*)

MOIRA: You can *both* hear the baby crying?

WILLIAM: Look what she's done to Moira! Our daughter's gone deaf from that squealing. Deaf!

MOIRA: Right *now*?

BONNIE: Oh, Moira, don't be morbid.

WILLIAM: Get's easier to handle after your second. *(He pours himself another stiff one.)*

BONNIE: Why do you always have to make a dark situation worse?

WILLIAM: What are you going on about?

BONNIE: You, always with that stupid bottle.

WILLIAM: This is a supreme cut of Brandy. I paid a lot of money for this brandy—

BONNIE: —A lot of OUR money—

WILLIAM: MY money. Those are MY pension checks coming in, you know.

BONNIE: Oh, here we go again...

(MOIRA climbs the stairs carefully while her parents argument dims into the kitchen quiet. [Full text in Addendum])

(She tiptoes across the upstairs hallway.)

(There are three doors upstairs. The Master Bedroom, MOIRA and Maeb's old room, and the bath. MOIRA opens the door to her old room.)

(It is dark.)

(The universe holds for one last moment before tipping irrevocably onto its head.)

(MOIRA turns on the light. She listens for her parents. She slowly steps towards the large, old fashioned bassinet. She peeks inside, digging around the blankets.)

(MOIRA stares, agape.)

MOIRA: All the hairs on my neck...

(BONNIE and WILLIAM stand in the doorway.)

BONNIE: Moira Angela Lane, you get away from that crib!

(MOIRA *stares.*)

MOIRA: Is this some kind of joke?

WILLIAM: Jesus, Bonnie, she's got such God awful pipes on her. Sure we can't keep her outside?

(MOIRA *lifts what can only be described as a doll out from the crib. Only, it's not a doll made of fabric and porcelain, but a doll made of twigs, and red yarn. There are no discernible features, but four limbs and a "head". She lifts the thing by its "leg".)*

MOIRA: Just what the hell are you two playing at here?

(BONNIE *answers with a scream.*)

BONNIE: Moira, put her down! My God, what is wrong with you? You give her to me right this second!

(BONNIE *rescues the "baby" from* MOIRA's *careless grasp and cradles it.*)

BONNIE: Maeb! Oh sweet lord in heaven. Are you alright? *(She tenderly checks the "baby" over.)*

(WILLIAM *claps his hands to his ears.*)

WILLIAM: You've gone and done it now, haven't you? There'll be no settling her after this.

BONNIE: Get out of my house!

MOIRA: What?

BONNIE: You heard me!

MOIRA: You can't possibly expect me to leave *now*—

BONNIE: I surely can! Shiva the Destroyer, you are!

WILLIAM: Ah, let her alone Bonnie, she's barren.

MOIRA: I'm not— What? Barren?

WILLIAM: I'm just saying is all—

BONNIE: What does that have to do with anything?

MOIRA: —I'm *not* barren—

WILLIAM: Just that she's a bit dim on the subject of child rearing is all.

BONNIE: William, you don't have to be a genius to know better than to be swinging babies around by their ankles!

WILLIAM: I'm just saying—

MOIRA: That's not a baby!

BONNIE: You're both mad! The pair of you. You make me sick.

MOIRA: My God, you're serious—

BONNIE: Get out of my sight!

MOIRA: But…

Moira tries to make sense of things…

BONNIE: *OUT!*

WILLIAM: *(Softly to* MOIRA*)* Come on, let her simmer tonight, she'll be stew by morning.

(WILLIAM *escorts* MOIRA *out of the room.)*

(BONNIE *bounces and hums to the baby.)*

(MOIRA *feels, for the moment, that she has gone mad.)*

(*She doesn't like the feeling.)*

(*She doesn't like it at all.)*

(*Black)*

Scene 4

(*The next day)*

(*All the shades are open. Unfortunately, the sky outside has decided to hide and the dirt seems to have grown. Wind and a spatter of rain rattles the panes.)*

(*Dim light creeps into the house.)*

(WILLIAM *reads his book on the porch.*)

(MOIRA *makes breakfast. She makes a perfectly ordered breakfast, full of rhyme and reason. Everything makes sense again, down to the last fork.*)

(*She contemplates her masterpiece.*)

WILLIAM: It's too dark.

MOIRA: What?

WILLIAM: I said it's too damn dark. (*He thumps down his book and shuffles into the kitchen.*)

WILLIAM: Goddamned strangest weather. Like the sun plumb fell out of the sky.

MOIRA: Do you want some coffee?

WILLIAM: I don't drink coffee.

MOIRA: You only pee in the mugs…

WILLIAM: What?

MOIRA: Nothing.

WILLIAM: Too dark to read, too dark to sit. What's that smell?

MOIRA: Breakfast.

WILLIAM: I'll have orange juice.

(MOIRA *pours juice.*)

WILLIAM: You didn't make crepes did you?

MOIRA: French toast and eggs.

WILLIAM: Ach, french toast, you're killing me. Why don't you tap a vein already and just bleed me dry.

MOIRA: I don't know how to make crepes.

WILLIAM: Any sign of your mother? I haven't heard her hooves this morning.

MOIRA: I don't think she's up yet.

(WILLIAM *slurps his juice.*)

(MOIRA *slurps her coffee.*)

MOIRA: Dad, when did Mom bring… "Maeb", home?

WILLIAM: Oh, I don't know, thing's about three months old now, I think, so that's what… June or thereabouts.

MOIRA: And did something…did mom maybe slip and fall first, or have a stroke, anything like that?

WILLIAM: Ach, you're a right ray of sunshine this morning.

MOIRA: Or it doesn't have to be an accident. I mean, has she started drinking or taking anything… Has she been on any new pills maybe? New medications?

WILLIAM: No. Hasn't been to the doctor in I don't know how long. Healthiest she's been in years. In fact, I don't think the woman's been sick since…

MOIRA: Since when?

(WILLIAM *thinks about Maeb. It fills him with a primal uncertainty.*)

(*He doesn't like it.*)

WILLIAM: Moira, I don't understand where you're going with this—

MOIRA: I'm just trying to find out why she's acting so… out of the ordinary.

WILLIAM: When has your mother *ever* been "ordinary?"

MOIRA: Well, what about the car? When did she do that? That's pretty unusual.

WILLIAM: Ai, the car again! What do I look like, her date book? How am I supposed to remember every fool thing she's up to? One day it ate gas, the next it was buggered. Christ Almighty. I thought you said there was breakfast.

MOIRA: I thought we'd wait for mom.

WILLIAM: Oh, so you want to be Little Miss Manners after last night, do ya? Well go ahead, detective. Be polite as punch. I'm hungry.

(MOIRA *hands* WILLIAM *the french toast and eggs.*)

WILLIAM: Where's the bacon?

MOIRA: There wasn't any.

WILLIAM: Damnit Moira, I thought I smelled bacon.

MOIRA: Well you didn't!

(WILLIAM *contemplates* MOIRA.)

(*He begins to eat.*)

WILLIAM: Where you been, Moira?

MOIRA: What?

WILLIAM: Been a long time, don't even see you at Christmas anymore.

MOIRA: Things are…things got, it was challenging. I have a lot to do at work, I just couldn't get away.

WILLIAM: They make you work on Christmas?

MOIRA: I was still, I'm still taking care of things. The house, it's all paid up—

WILLIAM: Ach, I know business is… That's not what I'm asking, that. Been hard, is all. Not seeing you. Loosing one daughter is, hard enough, but you been gone so long, feels like I lost you both. 'Course, you're off conquering the world, suppose it's been a sight more appealing than…this.

(MOIRA)

(MOIRA)

MOIRA: Dad, I—

WILLIAM: Didn't ask me about the name, you know.

MOIRA: What?

WILLIAM: Maeb. Your mother didn't ask me. Decided it all up on her own, that reincarnated stuff… Don't think she's ever forgiven herself about your sister. People of all sorts saying it was "God's plan" and bringing us casseroles. Nice enough mind you, but don't do much once a mind is made up.

MOIRA: You think she feels guilty?

WILLIAM: Maybe. Could be she sees this as a new start. Could be why she went out there fornicating like a feral cat. Could be if I think about it like that I forgive her a little. Big breach of trust, a thing like this. Raising another man's baby…ach, not everyone could do it.

MOIRA: Dad, that's not a baby.

WILLIAM: Oh, she's monstrous enough aright, but sometimes when your mother don't know it I go up and have a peek. Babies have a way of softening your insides.

(BONNIE *can be heard coming down the stairs.*)

WILLIAM: 'Course, you ever tell your mother I said all that, I'll disown you. (*He picks up his plate and heads to the porch.*)

(BONNIE *passes* WILLIAM *in the living room.*)

BONNIE: Where are you off to?

WILLIAM: None of your damn business, that's where. And your daughter made us breakfast. Try not to bite into her too hard, eh?

(BONNIE *heads into the kitchen.*)

(WILLIAM *sits on the porch and eats french toast while imagining crepes.*)

(BONNIE *and* MOIRA)

BONNIE: Smells alright.

MOIRA: There's no bacon.

BONNIE: You made coffee?

MOIRA: You want some?

BONNIE: Did you wash out the mugs?

MOIRA: I found some in the back of the cupboard, I figured they were safe.

BONNIE: Ai, yeah then.

(MOIRA *pours a cup of coffee for* BONNIE.)

BONNIE: Don't know what your father's thinking peeing in 'em like that. Empties 'em out every couple days, fills 'em back up. I tried sneaking them out, fill 'em with water. Lord, did I hear it then.

(MOIRA *imagines a peaceful happy feeling.*)

BONNIE: Don't suppose you thought of breaking out the jam?

MOIRA: Oh—

BONNIE: I'll get it. (*She takes the jam out of the fridge.*) You did a nice job on the table.

MOIRA: Thanks.

BONNIE: I don't think we've used these dishes in ages.

MOIRA: Well, I thought it might be nice—

BONNIE: Apology accepted.

MOIRA: That's very…apology?

BONNIE: I thought about things and I guess I didn't figure what a frightful day it must have been for you, what with all the travel and then your father loosing his mind, peeing all over the place—

MOIRA: Mh-hm.

BONNIE: Course, you can't blame me for being a little off, myself, left to take care of a senile old man and a

tiny baby all as I am. But you were in a bit of a shock,
and I have to judge that fairly.

MOIRA: Thanks.

BONNIE: You're welcome. Besides babies is like rubber
at that age anyway, nature's version of a warranty.
Why, when you were little I must have dropped you
on your head a half dozen times. And look at you,
a lawyer! Course, I suppose you'll be wanting an
explanation. Seems a right awful thing not to know the
whole story of your sister's reincarnation when it's as
wondrous as it is. Can you pass me the butter?

(MOIRA does.)

BONNIE: I've been taking walks. Wonderful, long
walks in the woods. Don't know what took me so
long…perhaps it was knowing how your sister used
to love them what made me afraid. Afraid to go
out there by myself, enjoy myself in her woods. But
now, well. There's peace out there. Peace that's been
eluding man since the dawn of time. It's the trees, as
if they're looking down on us with pity, "Paur little
humans, their minds be so fraught with worries"
(they're Olde English, you know). And it was just after I'd
started going out there that I started feeling they were
whispering to me, right out of one of them faery tails
my mum would tell us when we were little.
Course, most of the stories she was telling were meant
for frighting, "If you steal cream in the morning, the
faeries will get ya", and so on, but this was different.
This was something… sacred. They were communing
with me, so I took to having longer and longer walks
and it weren't long after that I started feeling a
different sort of presence. Real heavy like, and magic.
Singular.
I started bringing honey with me. Mum used to say
they like honey. And I'd leave offerings. I wanted to let

him know I was enjoying the woods just the same as him. Oh, I could tell it was a him, there was something so… oaken about his weight. Sometimes I'd take a seat and he would settle all around me, holding me, and I'd stroke that honey bottle and give a little squeeze, and the whole of him would shiver. God, it was beautiful.

WILLIAM: *(Hollering)* Is there anymore of that sorry-excuse-for-French-cooking left?

BONNIE: *(Hollering back)* Why don't you come in here and see for yourself, you old goat. *(She catches herself, listens for Maeb.)* God, sometimes your father makes me loose my mind! Always yelling, it's contagious.

(WILLIAM enters the kitchen.)

BONNIE: Why are you always yelling?

WILLIAM: S'pose I want to be heard.

MOIRA: The toast is on the stove.

WILLIAM: Don't suppose you stirred up some bacon?

MOIRA: I told you already, there isn't any bacon in the house.

WILLIAM: Just doesn't seem like much of a breakfast without bacon.

BONNIE: Ach, Willy, you know there's no bacon! Why you going on about it? Leave her alone already.

WILLIAM: You playing at being friends this morning?

BONNIE: I don't know what you're talking about.

(WILLIAM helps himself to more toast.)

BONNIE: Where was I?

(MOIRA opens her mouth—)

BONNIE: Oh, right. The honey—

WILLIAM: Jesus Christ.

BONNIE: What now?

WILLIAM: You going on about them woods again? Lies, lies, and more lies!

BONNIE: I told you—

WILLIAM: Ain't no cloud in the woods fucking you on a bed of honey what makes a baby out of it!

MOIRA: Dad!

WILLIAM: What? She hadn't gotten to that part yet?

BONNIE: You think you're so clever don't you, insulting me every chance you get?

WILLIAM: Ain't nothing clever about it. It's factual.

BONNIE: Oh, go eat your toast and stay out of things!

(WILLIAM *grumbles and shuffles out.*)

BONNIE: And try not to choke on it this time!
I'll tell you one thing that Fleur was good for was keeping him off of my hump. Practically didn't speak to one another for two months. Not one word. Best two months of my life, I tell you that. More coffee?

(MOIRA *extends her cup and* BONNIE *fills it.*)

MOIRA: Listen, Mom, I was thinking I'd head into town today. I'm sure I can find a cab if I walk in a ways, I could come back here, get us a ride in?

BONNIE: What do you need me to go with you for?

MOIRA: I just thought it might be nice.

BONNIE: Oh?

MOIRA: Yes.

(BONNIE *regards* MOIRA *with a suspicious eye.*)

MOIRA: We could, maybe we could go shopping.

BONNIE: Mmm.

MOIRA: Might be nice. Bring dad along. We could get some bacon.

BONNIE: One big happy family?

(*Beat*)

MOIRA: Yes.

(BONNIE *takes her frustration out on the dishes.*)

BONNIE: Ach, I should have known. Making breakfast and letting me go on about my walks…

MOIRA: What are you—

BONNIE: —Meanwhile you're just scheming away—

MOIRA: —It's not a conspiracy!

BONNIE: Oh no? You're not, what, planning on dropping us off at a funeral parlour while we're out?

MOIRA: No. Jesus.

BONNIE: Willy? Twigs thinks we should all ride into town together, just for kicks. One big happy family. What do you think about that? (*To* MOIRA) Why don't you just go on and tell me what you're aiming for Twiggy, save the indecency of playing at me like I'm a child.

MOIRA: Fine. I think you should see a doctor. I think you and dad are losing your minds and I want you to see a doctor. I'll take care of all the expenses—

BONNIE: Oh, you're a shiner, you are. My own flesh and blood. (*She heads into the living room.*)

(MOIRA *follows.*)

BONNIE: Daughter knows best, eh? Come here to save us did you?

MOIRA: Stop twisting everything around. I'm just concerned—

BONNIE: Our daughter wants to put us away, what do you think of that Willy?

MOIRA: No one said anything/ about putting you away—

BONNIE: /Willy, I'm talking to you…

(WILLIAM *stands frozen, staring out the door.*)

MOIRA: Dad?

(WILLIAM *turns around, he has wet his pants.*)

WILLIAM: I saw it.

BONNIE: Willy, what on earth?

WILLIAM: I saw your damn cloud. (*He starts to fall.*)

(MOIRA *steps in to catch* WILLIAM.)

MOIRA: Oh my God, dad? Dad?

(WILLIAM *stutters.*)

(BONNIE *looks outside with eager eyes.*)

BONNIE: Oh Moira, do you think he's come to see the baby?

(*Black*)

Scene 5

(*There's no telling what time of day it is, for the house is besieged by horrible weather.*)

(*The upstairs bedroom*)

(WILLIAM *is in bed, a mountain of pillows behind him.* MOIRA *wets a wash cloth and dabs at his face.*)

(*After a while,* BONNIE *comes in, hair blown about, shoes muddy, she's all a twitter.*)

BONNIE: Oh, Moira, Moira, me, where's he gone do you think?

MOIRA: Shhh! Dad's asleep. Where have you been?

BONNIE: Can't imagine he would come all the way here just to make your father piss his pants. You don't think Willy was rude to him, do you? Said anything strange? And Lord, what a storm. Is he angry maybe?

MOIRA: You need to stay with dad while I go for help.

BONNIE: What?

MOIRA: He needs a doctor.

BONNIE: You're in the middle of experiencing something here, a real damn miracle, and you want to go and invite science inside? *(She smells the air.)* God, I can still smell him. He's not far off.

MOIRA: Stop it! Stop flitting around like that. Dad's sick!

(But BONNIE is listening to another channel.)

BONNIE: You know it wasn't like your father said. Her coming. There wasn't any *intercourse*. A presence like that, he doesn't deign to take our shape... It would be like you or me trading our skin for a parasite's. No, when he came unto me it was like a great rushing wind. And I knew. I knew that he had blessed us with a child. Your father just can't wrap his pea sized brain around it. Never did have much faith in the way of things beyond us. Couldn't understand it when your sister died, why he wasn't as angry as I was with God. Then I came to realize, it's because he never much believed in Him to begin with. Never much believed in anything he couldn't touch with his hands. Do you think I should put a dress on little Maeb?

(MOIRA and her frustration)

MOIRA: No, I do not think you should put that thing in a dress! I need you to concentrate here. Now is not time for one of your fits. I need you to focus!

(BONNIE touches MOIRA's furrowed brow.)

BONNIE: I remember when the doctors first told us she wasn't long for this world, you put on that wrinkled brow and sat right down next to her bed. I knew there was no moving you. By her bed for weeks! I never even saw you use the toilet. I thought "That's it, I'm going to lose them both. One's dying and the other is turning to stone." You're father is old, Moira. But you, you're missing everything!

MOIRA: Mom, please. Dad could be having a stroke. I have to go out to the main road and try and get a signal—

BONNIE: Stroke! What stroke? He's just fainted is all.

(BONNIE *slaps* WILLIAM *on his pale, sweaty, face.*)

BONNIE: Hey, Willy, open your eyes. You're scaring your daughter.

MOIRA: Stop that, what's the matter with you?

(WILLIAM *opens his eyes.*)

WILLIAM: Ach.

BONNIE: Ai, there he is, see. Stop being dramatic. *(She leans into him.)* Hey, Willy, where'd he go? Where'd he go, Willy?

MOIRA: Give him some room, Jesus.

WILLIAM: Moira…

MOIRA: Yeah dad?

WILLIAM: Bring me my cups.

MOIRA: What? No, dad, I'm going to go for a doctor—

WILLIAM: My cups!

BONNIE: Typical. TYPICAL, asking for a fool thing like that.

MOIRA: Be quiet! He's sick, and you need to be nice to him. You need to stay here with him while I go for help!

BONNIE: I am not sitting next to him and that filth—

MOIRA: Yes, you damn well *will*—

BONNIE: Ach, stop trying to tell me what to do!

WILLIAM: *(Mustering strength)* Bring 'em to me! Set 'em round the bed, will ya?

MOIRA: Dad, you need help—

BONNIE: But Willie, *where'd he go?*

MOIRA: Leave him alone, for Christ's sake!

BONNIE: Willie—

MOIRA: Look, dad—

WILLIAM: *(Thunder and brass)* Get the cups! The cups! The cups!

*(*MOIRA *takes a breath.)*

MOIRA: Fuck. Fine, but then I'm going for some fucking help! *(She storms towards the door.)*

WILLIAM: Good. Good girl. *(He closes his eyes again.)*

*(*BONNIE *blocks the exit.)*

BONNIE: Oh, you'll bloody well listen to him about his stupid cups, but I can't have the time of day with you?

MOIRA: Move.

BONNIE: It's always been that way, the two of you… peas in a pod—never could get a word in edgewise. Like living in a foreign country where everyone got the punch lines but never let you in on the jokes.

WILLIAM: Bonnie—

BONNIE: It was always your sister, God rest her soul, who understood me. She cared. Then God went and

stole her from me, and I'm left with the pair of you.
Whispering, ganging up on me…

MOIRA: No one is ganging up on you.

BONNIE: Oh no? Oh NO?

MOIRA: We don't have time for one of your tantrums—

BONNIE: Right. What am I thinking, standing here
talking. We've got to get your father's fancy cups.

(BONNIE *storms down the stairs,* MOIRA *follows…*)

WILLIAM: Moira?

MOIRA: It's fine, dad.

(MOIRA *senses that the tiny tear in the universe is back. It
has sucked the light from the downstairs.*)

(*In the dark,* BONNIE *has found one of* WILLIAM's *cups and
hurls it against the ground with a CRASH.*)

(WILLIAM *sits up at the shattering porcelain.*)

WILLIAM: What was that?

MOIRA: I don't know, just stay put. Mom, what are you
doing?

(*CRASH*)

(MOIRA *makes her way to a lamp and switches it on.*)

(*The earth has moved into the corners and crevices, it's
started to work it's way up the stairs.*)

MOIRA: Jesus Christ!

WILLIAM: Bonnie, you better not be breaking 'em! (*He
and his blanket head unsteadily towards the door.*)

MOIRA: (*Calling out*) Dad, I can handle this.

WILLIAM: No, you bloody well can't. Bonnie! Ya old
bitch, stop breaking things!

BONNIE: Oh, shut it, you! Sitting around like a ripe auld king. People've got other things to tend to you know, than you and your stupid cups.

MOIRA: Stop, stop it! You need to stop playing this sick game! Why would you bring all this dirt in here?

(BONNIE *laughs.*)

BONNIE: You think I did this?

MOIRA: Yes.

(BONNIE *laughs harder.*)

(WILLIAM *makes it down the last of the stairs and wrestles with* BONNIE *for one of his cups.*)

WILLIAM: Have you gone mad? What are you doing?

(*It splashes everywhere.*)

(WILLIAM *stutters, desperate.*)

WILLIAM: No!

(BONNIE *and* WILLIAM *fight for a second, and a third… she works her way through the remaining cups under the following.* MOIRA, *at some point, enters the wrestling match.*)

BONNIE: (*Overlapping*) Mad? Mad? I'll tell what's mad is your bumbling, no good for anything, brandy-swilling self, coming after me, asking me to have anything to do with your filthy habits. I'm tired of it Willy, I'm tired of pretending they're not here, stinking the place up. Moira comes in asking about you and I think to myself, what can it hurt? But then you're here, barely breathing, and you want not to be with me, or the baby, but to be with your disgusting pots of piss! I'll not have it any more!

WILLIAM: (*Overlapping*) Stop it! I've a right to it, same as…goddamnit Bonnie, you have no idea what your… that's mine to be doing with! Wouldn't expect you to understand a man's magic— Give that to me you crazy auld bitch!

MOIRA: *(Overlapping)* Stop it! Both of you, Jesus Christ! …I can't take it anymore… Dad, you need to— Give me that—you're both acting like children!

(The last cup splashes it's contents across MOIRA*'s face.)*

(Everyone freezes.)

*(*MOIRA*'s rage.)*

(The house shivers.)

(Thump…)

WILLIAM: Goddamnit, now you've gone and let things in…

(THUMP!)

*(*MOIRA *makes up her mind.)*

MOIRA: You're both sick. Do you hear me? SICK! *(She marches to the door.)*

WILLIAM: Moira, don't!

(It opens with a SNAP, hitting her square in the head.)

(A small mountain of dirt moves in to catch her as she drops, unconscious, to the ground.)

(Black)

END OF ACT ONE

(During intermission, windows and doors should be opened to let in as much earth as possible. The occasional root or leaf joins the party. This earthly migration may continue during BONNIE*'s monologue and throughout the rest of the play as befitting the scenes.)*

ACT TWO

Scene 1

(A bell tolls.)

(Upstairs BONNIE *has thrown the windows open wide and sits in a rocking chair in the middle of it all, singing a faery song and rocking little Maeb with the wind.)*

(Mid-stairs WILLIAM *sits sleeping, his blanket and porcelain fragments around him for comfort.)*

*(*MOIRA *lies as she fell, left to seed in the earth wrapped around her like a pillow. Shadows tug at her consciousness.)*

(The bell)

BONNIE: When I was little, there weren't such a thing as science getting in the way of the world. If you thought you saw a spirit, you probably did. None of this "Let's get a doctor on you" business. People's minds were more open to possibility. Why, I remember reading in my Encyclopedia that the Earth gave birth to the moon. They thought it true enough to write it, print it, and even draw up an illustration, and so how come Moira wants to come marching in here questioning such a miracle as you?

(The bell)

BONNIE: Things have a way of revealing themselves and when they do you have to be asking yourself "Am I going to stand here, in the mud, legs wooden and unbendable, or am I the kind of person who can turn, change perspective, and keep moving?" I was the kind who wanted to keep moving. Your sister? She's the kind that can't look but straight ahead. Don't matter which way the wind blows her, she'll keep her nose down to the track she's been following, even while the scenery changes around her. It's the miracles in life you have to cling to. That girl down there, she don't know what I know. She don't understand that life's full of funny business.

(The bell. BONNIE *talks to the wind.)*

BONNIE: She's beautiful, don't you think? Rosy cheeks… Healthy appetite. You should be proud of her. She's perfect. Course, a mother always thinks so. It's the father that's left to reconcile his seed with the face staring up at him. Must be damn hard to be left out of the baking. I know every curve, every freckle, every hair on her head. I drew dreams around my belly and gave her the best parts…a mother is always mothering even when she's doing the wash. But you can see what wonder you done, can't you? What wonder…

(The bell)

BONNIE: Wee little nose, and her wee little ears… I didn't know you was gifting me with a second chance. That moment, I was so filled up with you…I had no idea the joy that was coming. You know, we didn't know what to do with her the first time. She came along and Moira was just starting to take care of herself, and I'd given away all Moira's things. So we put her in the woodbox till we could afford another crib, only she liked it so much we never did get one. I knew then that she was special. One foot in this world, and one in yours.

(The bell)

(Downstairs a wind ruffles MOIRA's *hair and she stirs in the mud.)*

BONNIE: Moira took to her like a little mother. Which was good enough, me being as frightened as I was. And Maeb never faulted me for it, never begrudged me the milk that dried up. Never looked at me with the same eyes as Moira, like she knew I wasn't worthy. William, always telling me what to do, and then Moira, taking over Sunday breakfasts…

(The bell)

BONNIE: But Maeb, bless her heart, would sit by my bed when I didn't want to leave it, and sing. I always felt better by that voice of hers. I should have, I should have told her that more. *(She thinks about this.)*

(The bell)

BONNIE: T'were an awful punishment to be left with them two downstairs, you know. Always looking at me with judgment—trying to digest their disappointment. And Moira, the little mother, swallowing every last drop of grief, until there wasn't no more left in the world and all I could do was cry dry, crunchy tears.

(The bell)

*(*MOIRA *opens her eyes. She feels her head.)*

MOIRA: Mom?

BONNIE: Don't you think she looks a bit like her though? Sisters do share a tie that doesn't shake. Even all this time passed and I can't look at one but see the other. She was so frail and shriveled up the last time I saw her. Terrible thing to be, eaten away at, like she was… And Moira sitting by her, always sitting by her, not letting me alone with her, in case she missed a beat.

(The bell)

*(*MOIRA *tries to understand the damage around her.)*

BONNIE: No, I know you could have…if I'd only listened better, maybe…but the time, it went so quickly, days even it seemed, a few hours and then minutes, and then seconds it was between the doctor telling us and her breathing her last. I swear it wasn't but one of my heartbeats between the knowing and the dying, and yet I remember so many shades of weather…

(The bell)

*(*MOIRA *starts digging, digging, digging)*

BONNIE: She didn't make it as long as they predicted. William and me down at the bank, trying to take another mortgage on the house to pay for it… Moira pulling her hair out over tuition. Couldn't understand all that talk of money with her lying there so pale.

(The bell)

*(*MOIRA *heads to the kitchen.)*

BONNIE: Course, I'm telling you this so you know— know how thankful I am to you for bringing her back. And I know t'were a thing unusual—not to be taken for granted. I won't be letting the world take advantage of her again, I'd fight to the death to protect her if need be, make no mistake of that. Or in my understanding in the world of miracles. But right now, in this moment, I'm happy as ever I could be. And I just want to thank ye.

(The bell)

(The wind rustles.)

BONNIE: Thirteen bells on the witches hour toll. *(She looks up.)* What whispers this?

*(*MOIRA *storms towards the door with a large pot, and a ladle, or whatever other kitchen tools she could find.)*

(She starts scooping the dirt, wild-eyed, towards the door.)

MOIRA: Un-fucking-believable. Leaving me to seed in the dirt. I could use some help…with this.

(No one helps.)

MOIRA: Absolutely out of my…element here. I should have become a, a psychologist, or a construction worker, what with this…mess. I knew I was in for *something*, being gone so long—parents get old, houses get mice—but this, this is beyond… Do you know how expensive my shoes are Dad? But don't move a muscle…don't you stir from those steps, because Moira will take care of everything, just like always, just like I am forever taking care of you both… Just like I always had to take care of…every— Always making the tough call. To dig or not to dig, that is the—MOTHER! Will you put that basket of branches down for one moment and help me clean up the natural disaster in your living room? Mudslides! Alzheimer's or dementia I can deal with…but, oh, God, HELP ME GET RID OF THE DIRT!!

(MOIRA throws her "tools". Nothing is helping. The dirt is still coming. She surveys the damage. She needs something to shore up the door, and the windows…)

(She spins back to the kitchen.)

(WILLIAM stirs.)

WILLIAM: What in the bonny fuck is all that noise?

MOIRA: *(OS)* Dad?

WILLIAM: What are you doing?

(MOIRA rolls the kitchen table towards the door.)

MOIRA: The door won't close.

(WILLIAM watches.)

MOIRA: You could help me, you know.

(WILLIAM and his hands.)

WILLIAM: Won't do no good.

MOIRA: Sure it will, we'll get this boarded up, someone is bound to notice there's been a…a landslide. They'll come.

WILLIAM: Won't do no good.

(More dirt crumbles in through the windows.)

(MOIRA surveys the shelves.)

WILLIAM: Not my books!

MOIRA: I'll buy you some new ones.

WILLIAM: Goddamnit Moira, you should have taken me away like I'd asked. I told you… Now everything's off. Can't you feel it? I said stay away from my books!

(A tug of war)

MOIRA: Fine! Take your precious books. Your pictures. Your cups! What do I care?

(MOIRA throws the books at WILLIAM, she sweeps the rest off the shelves.)

MOIRA: You're crazy, and you smell like piss. And when all this is cleaned up…when I'VE cleaned everything up, I'm putting you both in a home, because you're out of your damned ancient minds! *(She searches for other items to stuff in the windows.)*

WILLIAM: Never understood where you got your will from. Strong as oak, even now. Sometimes you're so damn stoic…Jesus, Moira, these are my things. Little pieces of a life used up. Weren't never nothing much, but t'were mine good enough. Can't be expecting you to understand, or that broken woman upstairs what's gone and mixed things up. Everything was alright for a while. Wasn't a thing normal in the house, but at least the brain and the mouth, sending signals to the tongue to "Speak kindly"… curl up the corners of the mouth when people visit sweetness upon your step… at least all of that was still functioning—

MOIRA: Uh-huh.

(WILLIAM looks at his broken pieces of cup.)

WILLIAM: There's dark happenings stirring this pot tonight, and I don't want to be a party to it any longer.

(MOIRA stomps into the kitchen to looks for more tools.)

WILLIAM: We killed her, you know. Maeb. Between our arguing, and our hating, it turned black inside her precious open heart, and I know it was that what done her in. Every day I go repenting for the evils I said, the abscesses I created…I never expected to make it this long with that woman. Maybe if I'd loved her right, like I was supposed to… Never understood why God steered me to her, like a lost ship she was—been tossing in the waves long before I met her… and I took charge of it without knowing. I tried though, I did try— But you can't be lying that long and not pay a price.

Never should have moved your mother into this wooded abyss, far away from it all… I thought it would help. I thought… *(He looks to his hands.)* These impotent hands…what good did I ever make of 'em?

(Shadows peek.)

(WILLIAM begins eating the porcelain chips.)

(The wind)

WILLIAM: One for the woman I couldn't love enough. One for the child turned so weak and grey. One for the daughter suffering our burdens to carry. One for the house falling in around us. One for the man who couldn't…wouldn't see.

(MOIRA)

(WILLIAM)

MOIRA: Dad?

WILLIAM: We did this.

MOIRA: Jesus Christ, what did you do?

WILLIAM: We killed her Moira. Your mother and—
There was a, a poison…that I, I didn't—I was marking
the days as she marked the breaths.

MOIRA: What are you talking about?

WILLIAM: Your sister just lying there so pale… And
now she's come back to haunt. She used to love those
long walks, just like your mother, talking to them
woods…and now she's here—

MOIRA: Listen to me, that is not Maeb.

WILLIAM: Oh, but it's something isn't it? Looking to
collect on ills past-due, dark and fearsome…I'm sorry
Moira. I was willing her to pass. With things so bad as
they were, up to our ears in medical bills… She was
only seventeen, Moira, so fragile. If I had willed her to
get better, do you think God would be punishing us
now?

MOIRA: This is not…Daddy? This is not God!

(BONNIE's *singing tinkles down the stairs.*)

WILLIAM: I'm sorry, Moira, you'll have to clean up the
pieces without me. But I think, I think I'm going to
sleep peaceful for the first time in years. (*He closes his
eyes.*)

(MOIRA *is a storm in herself. She rocks* WILLIAM, *the world
around them is shaking.*)

(BONNIE's *singing gets so loud that the place practically
vibrates with it.*)

(MOIRA *can't take it any longer.*)

MOIRA: MOTHER!

(MOIRA. *Her panic. The stairs*)

(BONNIE *keeps singing.*)

(MOIRA *scrambles up the stairs.*)

MOIRA: Will you answer me? (*She throws open the door to Maeb's bedroom.*)

(BONNIE *is rocking fervently.*)

BONNIE: Thirteen. Thirteen Moira. Something wicked, something fierce—

MOIRA: Daddy's dead.

(BONNIE *stops.*)

BONNIE: Willy?

MOIRA: He's dead.

(BONNIE)

(BONNIE)

BONNIE: Was that all?

MOIRA: What?

(*But* BONNIE *is not talking to* MOIRA.)

BONNIE: Thirteen bells… The price of a child… Taken like that?

MOIRA: He killed himself. Don't you see?

(*The house*)

(*The shadows*)

(*The wind*)

MOIRA: We've got to, we've got to get out of here.

BONNIE: I don't think so, Twigs.

MOIRA: Where's your coat?

BONNIE: Things stirring deep beneath me, beneath the crust of the earth on which we stand, boiling from the bowels of time itself…from my bones—

MOIRA: Okay, fuck the coat.

(MORIA *reaches after her.*)

BONNIE: You don't see Moira. He's angry.

MOIRA: Who? Your cloud? You're crazy! It's the weather, it's dumping outside and we need to get out of this damned ancient house—

(BONNIE *shakes herself loose.*)

BONNIE: Ripples. A million ripples… This is us. Stop looking at me like that, I am NOT GOING ANYWHERE. None of us is going anywhere. This is the time, this is the place, to reckon with God.

MOIRA: I can't do this! Time opening up into a massive…I can't, what do you want me to… Have you heard anything I've said? Dad is DEAD.

BONNIE: I heard you. Of course I heard you. I've been living with that man the whole of my adult life, you think I didn't hear you? That it didn't *land*? I'm telling you this is bigger than that. Bigger than you or me— Maeb came with a…some kind of…a price I didn't… understand. A tangle. And you're in it. You're smack dab in the middle of it! Why are you here Moira? Why are you here, fucking things up?

MOIRA: I came for YOU!

(MOIRA *clocks* BONNIE *in the jaw.* BONNIE *falls to the ground in a heap.*)

(MOIRA *drags her towards the door and down the steps, but the earth has filled in the living room.*)

(*There is no way out.*)

(*Lightening and…dark*)

Scene 2

(A little while later…)

(A music box plays.)

(A hurricane lamp starts to flicker, bringing the shadows with it.)

(MOIRA has made her way into the attic via a pull-down ladder in the hall of the second floor.)

(It is dusty, it is dim, it holds on to the things we do not want to look at, but cannot bear to throw away.)

(MOIRA peers into the music box on the floor, various open boxes scattered around her.)

(She feels the weight of things left stewing.)

(It doesn't let her breathe.)

(Below her, BONNIE stirs.)

BONNIE: Moira?

(The music box stops. MOIRA shakes it.)

(Nothing)

(Wind)

MOIRA: Up here.

BONNIE: Where?

MOIRA: Upstairs…

(Whisper)

(Staring)

BONNIE: What upstairs, up stairs to where?

MOIRA: In the attic. Scrambling for…something…

BONNIE: What?

(MOIRA and the hurricane lamp gape down at her.)

MOIRA: I'm up here, Mom.

BONNIE: Ach, watch that light! I've got a mighty headache.

(MOIRA *stares.*)

MOIRA: Are you alright?

BONNIE: I just told you my damn head hurts!

(MOIRA *looks at* BONNIE, *her mind playing catch up.*)

(*Eventually…*)

BONNIE: Well, have you gone and left your body to hang there all night staring at me like a sack of meat, or what? I told you, turn down the lamp!

MOIRA: Okay.

(MOIRA *and the lamp descend.*)

BONNIE: What in the bonny fuck are you doing up in the attic, anyway?

MOIRA: I was thinking—

BONNIE: No.

MOIRA: Excuse me?

BONNIE: You thinking has never led to anything good—

(MOIRA *heads into the bathroom.*)

BONNIE: —and there ain't nothing up there what needs disturbing!

MOIRA: (*OS*) *I've been thinking*, that daddy might have some rope or something in the attic, something sturdy. We'll climb out the window, escape all of, this, and head back to something…normal.

BONNIE: Ha!

MOIRA: (*OS*) Why is that funny?

BONNIE: Can't hardly walk without feeling every creak and moan, now you want me to go jumping out windows?

(MOIRA *returns with a wet towel for* BONNIE'*s head.*)

MOIRA: You're not nearly as feeble as you like people to think.

BONNIE: You should know that better than most, I suppose.

MOIRA: What's that supposed to mean?

BONNIE: Nearly dead by your hand, and now you want to be playin' "Guess Who?"

MOIRA: You're not nearly/ dead.

BONNIE: /What in the hell were you thinking hitting me like that?

MOIRA: You were hysterical.

BONNIE: And I suppose you were calm as silk.

MOIRA: No. No, I'm not saying that. *(Beat)* Mom, dad is—

BONNIE: —Where's Maeb?

MOIRA: What?

BONNIE: Maeb! Maeb, your sister! What did you do with her?

MOIRA: I, nothing—

BONNIE: Moira Angela Lane, if you hurt one hair on her head— *(She runs to the baby's room and gently lifts "Maeb" out of the cradle.)* —Oh, thank heavens for small miracles. Shush, shush little baby. Oh. Mamma's here. Oh.

(MOIRA *watches.*)

(*The hairs on the back of her neck stand at attention.*)

MOIRA: You probably shouldn't be walking around just yet.

BONNIE: Oh, leave off, Moira.

MOIRA: Things aren't, I mean, there's a… You should sit down.

BONNIE: I said leave off! Don't need you fussing over me like a babe. Poor thing needs feeding. Lying here all that time, on her lonesome because of you and your mighty fist.

MOIRA: *(Softly)* Is it mighty?

BONNIE: What are you going on about?

MOIRA: *(Muttering)* Words tilting…changing color… *(Then)* Something's gone strange, I can feel it.

BONNIE: Poor thing. She's hungry as can be after all that fuss!

(MOIRA laughs.)

BONNIE: Something funny?

MOIRA: *She's hungry?* Something is happening here, all *this*—pulsing…Dad's face echoing at me. And you want to play house?

BONNIE: You sure you haven't lost your marbles, Moy?

MOIRA: *My* marbles? Are you… No, you know what? Let's get your little "Maeb" there something to eat! What'll it be? Huh? Moss? Roots? Mud-pie? I'm afraid the kitchen is caved in, so choices are *limited*—

BONNIE: She'll have mother's milk, Moira.

MOIRA: Oh, my God! You can't be—

(BONNIE stares.)

MOIRA: You are, aren't you? You're serious! "Mother's milk"?

BONNIE: You know, you don't look the least bit attractive with your jaw hanging open like that—

MOIRA: You're going to go and stick your tit in that thing's, what? Does it even have a, a "mouth"?

(BONNIE bristles.)

BONNIE: You can spit in the face of any God you want Moira, but as long as you are a guest in my house you will show *some* respect for this miracle and the things you don't understand. *(She drapes a cloth over her shoulder in order to "feed" Maeb.)* Naught for nothing, is he here, Moira. We ought at least be civil while he figures these things out.

MOIRA: Right. "He." *(She turns on her heel and climbs back into the attic.)*

BONNIE: Where are you going? Leaving me in the dark? Come back here!

(MOIRA thumps the lamp down near the ladder, casting a muted glow on BONNIE and Maeb.)

(She kicks the music box into a corner, a box of clothes tilts and spills.)

MOIRA: Are you sure daddy didn't have a little corner up here all to himself? Somewhere he would have kept things? This all looks like your stuff.

BONNIE: What, in a house full of girls? He got the garage. What need would he have for an attic too?

MOIRA: So *nothing* up here belongs to him?

BONNIE: Well, I'm sure there are a few boxes what got lost in the shuffle. Right tantrum, you're throwing.

(MOIRA hunts.)

(BONNIE feeds.)

(Memories crowd.)

BONNIE: Shame about your father. He hated this house. Would never want to be buried here, in the front room. On the other hand, he's got his books. And that god forsaken couch—

MOIRA: Mother!

BONNIE: What? My head hurts. *(Beat)* Up there rooting and pillaging. Go ahead and weave yourself a ladder out of this mysterious rope you're hoping to find. I'm not leaving. I'm not leaving Maeb here on her lonesome. My little angel of solitude amongst all of this...*ugliness*. Deserves a fair chance is all. I'm not taking myself out of here like a coward, tail tucked between my legs.

MOIRA: Fine. You can strap it to your chest and jump—

BONNIE: Moira!

MOIRA: We can't stay here! If dragging that thing along is the only way to get you out of here, then so be it.

BONNIE: Such insipid—

MOIRA: What?

BONNIE: —hate. You have so much hatred inside you Moira!

MOIRA: This is about survival Mother, not hate. Escape—/ God, the fog of it all...

BONNIE: /Survival my arse. You're talking to the Queen of Survival. That's all I've been doing for the past thirty years, surviving. You think you're the one who has it rough? Maybe you have more time left to miss her, but you also have more time to heal. Older bones, they don't mend so fast. Injuries last longer, get harder to forget about. There you were, off to the races and passing the bar... Your father and I left alone to rot, in this place. The memory of your sister haunting my every teardrop. You want to talk about surviving?

MOIRA: No.

(BONNIE *scrambles up the ladder, Maeb and all.*)

BONNIE: Well, I do, I— Oh.

(BONNIE *stares at a memory in the shape of a wooden rocking horse.*)

BONNIE: Will you look at that? Will you look at that Twiggy?

(*Beat*)

(*Beat*)

MOIRA: It's, the air up here, it's not nice.

BONNIE: I should bring that down. She, remember she would laugh for hours on that…rocking, and singing, singing away with words we've forgotten. She spoke long before we could understand her, you know. Not like you. You were silent for twenty-three months, assessing everything, waiting till you learned just the right words to tell me how inadequate a mother you thought I was. I should bring it down for her—

(MOIRA *and the memories.*)

BONNIE: Moira?

MOIRA: Do you think he'd have a box, or just… There's too much *stuff* up here—

BONNIE: Moira, you're missing it!

MOIRA: What?

BONNIE: Memory lane. Can't you, for Christ's sake, stop puttering around over there and look at this!

MOIRA: It's an antique.

BONNIE: Help me bring it down.

MOIRA: I don't think so.

BONNIE: I'll dust it off, good as new. This attic is like a vault, nothing ever spoils up here. I tuck it away and

it's safe for all eternity. Look at that, not a splinter,
not an inch of rot. Good as the day I tucked it up here.
Here, you take the tail end—

MOIRA: I will not! I will not carry that colossus down so
you can perch your, *doll*, on top of it! *Where are daddy's
things?!*

(BONNIE *boils.*)

BONNIE: Always your father! ALWAYS HIM over ME.
Never a care, a thought what wasn't just *left over*…
Dead as doornails and you're still clamoring for his
lap! *(She tucks the now "sleeping" Maeb in an old basket in
order to tug at the rocking horse herself.)*

MOIRA: You're going to hurt yourself.

BONNIE: Don't flatter me. If I thought for one mighty
second that you actually cared…

(MOIRA *watches* BONNIE *struggle.*)

BONNIE: Always staring at me with the same look.
Irritation. Disgust. Shame. You know I was taking care
of myself just fine before you came along, and I was
gonna' be just fine after. You could have saved us all
of load of splinters if you just got down off that cross
you're always carrying.

MOIRA: I'm not, how dare YOU accuse ME of, of—
Jesus Christ!

BONNIE: Don't flatter yourself dear, he had much more
attractive hair.

(MOIRA *picks up the horse and heaves it down the stairs. It
lands with a sickening CRACK.)*

(BONNIE *stares in shock.)*

BONNIE: Jesus, Mary, and Joseph—

(MOIRA *looks around for more ammunition.)*

MOIRA: In all my years under this roof, I have NEVER, EVER, seen you exhibit even the remotest bit of kindness to anyone what didn't come from your own selfish designs. You stayed in bed, in your royal chambers, a wilting violet, for YEARS, and you still think that it's *me* who's out to get *you*? That I'M the one on the cross?!

BONNIE: Stop!

MOIRA: I cooked! I cleaned! I made daddy his lunches and paid the bills from *your* checkbook and got Maeb dressed for school, when she could go, all because you were too mired in your world of "Woe is me" to get out of bed, and you have the audacity to call *me* a martyr? That's YOU. THAT'S YOU BONNIE!

(The wind)

BONNIE: Those are my things!

MOIRA: This is junk!

BONNIE: You're going to wake her—

MOIRA: THAT'S NOT MAEB! That's not even a baby! You're insane, mom! You are out of your mind! Bonkers, crazy! A fucking cancer!

(BONNIE slaps MOIRA.)

(MOIRA)

(BONNIE)

(The wind)

MOIRA: Help me find some rope. *(She goes back to the boxes.)*

(BONNIE sniffles.)

BONNIE: There isn't anything out there for you but more of the same, Moira. He's here for a reckoning. Best be facing it dry and warm, rather than wet and shivering, that's a mother's advice for you, ungrateful little sow that you are I'll still tell you that.

MOIRA: That is exactly what I'm talking about— I'm trying to think practical and you're dreaming up faeries and dead daughters.

BONNIE: What dreaming? Look around you child, isn't a storm, this. Isn't a a storm at all. All the dirty little secrets just breathing and waiting…can't you feel their eyes, Moira?

MOIRA: Daddy, daddy, gone to pot, and you left here with me to haunt…

BONNIE: Can't you feel 'em 'gainst your back?

MOIRA: I don't feel anything!

(The wind)

BONNIE: Well I do, I feel it all. We're none of us clean Moira, and I'm only beginning just now to see it.

(MOIRA shivers despite herself.)

MOIRA: Look, I'm going to keep, looking around here—why don't, why don't you just…here, sit down. It's getting cold in here. Your face is…does it hurt? Where'd you put that washcloth?

BONNIE: He's whispering right now. Whispering things to me, such awful things.

MOIRA: Well, why don't you just try not to listen.

(MOIRA sits BONNIE down, wrapping her in a blanket, looking for the washcloth.)

BONNIE: You know I was nearly thirty-two when your father proposed?

MOIRA: Mhm.

BONNIE: Pregnant with you and nowhere else to go, I said yes. My mother and father were so relieved to

have me go. I wasn't one of those feminists, I wasn't
going to flush you away, pretend it never happened.

MOIRA: Thanks.

BONNIE: Though it did cross my mind a time or two…
just because I had no idea what to do with you. What
did I do with you?

(BONNIE *looks into* MOIRA.)

(MOIRA *looks into* BONNIE.)

(MOIRA *returns to her boxes.*)

MOIRA: You really should rest—

BONNIE: Selfishness. That's what I'm hearing Moira.
Was I a selfish mother?

MOIRA: I—

(*A box spills little girl's sheets across the floor. Delicate little
flowers and polka dots stare back.*)

(MOIRA *catches her breath as she lifts a sheet.*)

MOIRA: Jesus, she's everywhere.

(*The wind*)

MOIRA: Did you save everything she ever touched?

BONNIE: Ach, I asked you a question!

MOIRA: Yes.

BONNIE: Well?

MOIRA: I'm answering you. Yes.

BONNIE: Wh—

MOIRA: You damn well know you're selfish. Stop
asking me questions designed to start a fight, muddy
the matters— That wind! (*She takes a breath and lifts a
sheet from the box.*) Maybe we can…I can't believe you
saved all this. (*She pulls a few more sheets from the box,*

getting an idea. Under the following she starts tying the sheets together.)

(BONNIE *smells the past on the wind.)*

BONNIE: Well why wouldn't I want to save 'em? Perfectly good sheets, they are. And fresh as the day I tucked 'em away too. Remember how your sister loved to dance between the sheets? Four years old or sixteen, didn't matter, she'd have the biggest grin on her face, out there in the wind, fresh wash all 'round. Sick for weeks, and then… Sometimes I had to wash 'em twice just so she could dance while she was feeling good. Not a scent of selfish in that! *(Beat)* Do you remember, that concert…when you were…oh, I think you were twelve? You had practiced for weeks, you had a, what? A solo? We were all getting ready to pile into the car—

MOIRA: Maeb started throwing up. She got sick all over us.

BONNIE: You took your dress off right then and there, left it on the ground outside in the drive. Ran off to hide in one of your books.

MOIRA: I was twelve. We were always missing things. It wasn't her fault—

BONNIE: I did wash that very afternoon. Remember? I thought for sure she'd see the linens hanging and pop right up out of bed. How selfish is that? That's not— That's *love* Moira. I loved that girl more than anything. How could you think all I ever did for either of you was anything but love? Oh, how I wanted her to be there, to hear you sing.

MOIRA: You never *wanted* to go *anywhere*. If I needed a ride someplace, I always had to wait for daddy to get home. The day I got my license, I felt like I had won the lottery.

BONNIE: That's ridiculous. Of course I wanted to go places. I was just sick so often—

MOIRA: What are we— You want to rewrite the past *now*? *I don't want to go back there.* It's over, it's done. Let's just get out of here, away from this— *(She gathers her rope of sheets, heads for the ladder.)*

*(*BONNIE *stands in* MOIRA's *way.)*

BONNIE: No. I don't like the tone of your voice Miss Twigs. Not one iota! Recollections of things past so damned unwavering… If you think you can stand here and lecture me about how it went… You were the healthy one!/ Strong and stubborn, a world open to you and your blessed lungs. Are you trying to tell me that you think you got the short end of the stick? That somehow *you* should be pitied?// That life was UN-fair to YOU? Is that what you're saying?

MOIRA: /You think I don't know that? That I'm not thankful? //God, no. Why do you always have to twist *everything*—

*(*MOIRA *tries to get around her, but* BONNIE *grabs the other end of the sheets, pulling them to her.)*

BONNIE: Where have you been? Hmm?

MOIRA: Let go!

BONNIE: Where have you been? You want to talk about suffering—

MOIRA: —I'm trying NOT to talk about *any* of it—

BONNIE: —About how *rough* you had it, it's been eight years!

MOIRA: You're getting hysterical again!

BONNIE: Eight years you left us to rot. I want to know just what it is you've been up to that's so awful. Proof that *I* was so awful, that growing up here was *so awful*. You're a lawyer now, right? Can't have been all bad.

Then you go showing up in your fancy clothes, with your crisp speech, making me out to be some kind of… a villain—

MOIRA: Stop it!

BONNIE: WHERE HAVE YOU BEEN?

MOIRA: HIDING FROM YOU, from this place, from what I did…from all of—just, LET ME GO!

BONNIE: What *you* did? *(She lets go.)*

(MOIRA crashes into a stack of boxes, sending their contents scattering over top of her as she crumples to the ground.)

(A wire cage lands next to her, spraying straw and small bones everywhere.)

BONNIE: What did you do, Moira?

(A fresh cut on MOIRA's forehead sends a trickle of red stuff down her face.)

BONNIE: Look at me!

MOIRA: Leave me alone…

BONNIE: What did you do?

MOIRA: Nothing.

(BONNIE shakes MOIRA.)

BONNIE: TELL ME!

MOIRA: I, I don't— You're hurting me!

(But BONNIE can't stop…)

BONNIE: Moira! Moira, Moy! Tell me, girl, or so help me—

(The shadows spin.)

MOIRA: You wouldn't listen to reason! The doctors kept saying— She was practically translucent! Her eyes already fixed on something none of us could see…I held her hand as she fought to, *just to breathe,*

listening to you go on and on with the doctors
about experimental treatments, just eating up the
sympathy—

BONNIE: I didn't eat up—

MOIRA: Yes, you did! You were always, practically
smacking your lips with it. Stationed in front of a
doctor, or a nurse, anyone with a stethoscope, who
would applaud your "Brave little mother" routine—
She was in so much pain, and *dying*. And I *knew*. God,
I knew you would bankrupt us just to eke out a few
more selfish moments with that *shell* of my sister…
Nobody was speaking for *her*. I didn't— What else
could I have done, Mom? What more? What—

(MOIRA)

(Her hands)

MOIRA: —oh my God, what is—it's on my hands.

BONNIE: Moira!

(MOIRA looks closer at the debris.)

MOIRA: I… These are, bones…little…bones—

BONNIE: Tell me!

MOIRA: It's on my hands! *(She tries to wipe away the dust,
the tears, the bones…)*

(BONNIE reaches for MOIRA.)

BONNIE: WHAT DID YOU DO?

MOIRA: I, NOTHING! Get off of me! What is all this?!

(MOIRA wrestles herself free.)

*(BONNIE takes in MOIRA, the mess, her own white
knuckles.)*

(MOIRA)

(BONNIE)

(MOIRA)

BONNIE: It's a mess, is what it is. Look at you. Up here poking around like a pirate, you are. Stirring things… That bump on your head… We should get you cleaned up—

MOIRA: Ohmygodohmygod….

BONNIE: Moira you've had a shock, lucky to be forming sentences, you are. Never mind what they're about. Let's get you downstairs, you can lie down —

MOIRA: MOTHER!

BONNIE: Oh, Moira, look at you—always so *dramatic*, so *pale*…

(MOIRA)

(MOIRA)

(BONNIE *takes a breath.*)

BONNIE: It's nothing, it's… Your sister, bless her heart, asked for a bunny one Easter. That's all. Willy didn't think it good, what with her asthma, but, Maeb and I, she just had to have those rabbits, so one Sunday we snuck 'em in, just her and I. Named 'em Buster and Baby. Cutest damn things—

MOIRA: These are…this is more than just two rabbits—

BONNIE: I, when they died, I couldn't bear to…

(MOIRA *stares.*)

MOIRA: To what?

BONNIE: I just…kept replacing them.

(*Lightning*)

MOIRA: Jesus.

BONNIE: This is what I'm talking about! Look at how you're looking at me…so morbid. They were for your sister!

MOIRA: Maeb never said anything about rabbits!

BONNIE: It was a secret.

MOIRA: But… you, you just kept bringing rabbits up here to, what? Keep the dead ones company? What is WRONG with you?

BONNIE: Stop yelling at me!

MOIRA: No, I will not stop yelling at you! You have animal carcasses up here. Jesus, God, all my life I have had to, to clean up after you, but this? What in God's name were you thinking?

BONNIE: Well, I'm sure I wasn't— I, they were my, our little secret.

MOIRA: And nobody noticed? Not the sound or, the *smell*— My god the smell! But no…none of us knew, and you just kept bringing in rabbits—smuggling them into this wire coffin… There's no way that she—MAEB NEVER MENTIONED RABBITS… OhmyGodOhmyGodOhmyGOD… (*She starts tearing into other boxes, looking for more bones.*)

(BONNIE *shelters "Maeb".*)

BONNIE: You're crazed, stop knocking things about— Moira!

MOIRA: What else is lurking up here? What other horrors have you, *preserved*—pressed between pages, into the dust…Maeb would have told me. She told me everything! All the strange little pieces. Nothing fits, nothing fits!

(MOIRA *tears open box after box…hats, boxes of newspaper, a collection of creepy dolls and a box stuffed with pillows…*)

(*Items spill across the floor and down the ladder.*)

BONNIE: (*Overlapping*) Stop! Look what you're doing, you're terrifying her! Stirred her to crying, sweet innocent thing—Moira stop! (*She scoops Maeb up.*) Shh, shh. Shush little girl. I'm sorry. Mamma's sorry.

MOIRA: Rabbits and rabbits and death— The smell. Dust and bones and little bits of black pulling at my memory—

(*Another box tips, it's contents mixing with the dust and bones…*)

(*Bottles and jars of medicinal ilk go rolling. Syringes follow behind.*)

(MOIRA)

(MOIRA)

MOIRA: What on earth… (*She bends to pick them up.*)

BONNIE: (*Shrill*) Don't touch that!

MOIRA: Oh my God—

BONNIE: I said leave it alone!

MOIRA: But…

BONNIE: Moira!

MOIRA: Why do you have all this?

BONNIE: It's Maeb's medicines is all. I saved everything—

(*A bottle*)

(MOIRA *reads.*)

MOIRA: Skull and bones, and…Maeb wasn't diabetic, or—

BONNIE: Give that to me!

(BONNIE *tries to grab the bottles away from* MOIRA.*)

MOIRA: Some of these don't even have names on them…

BONNIE: They're old.

MOIRA: No, they don't have *names* on them. They haven't been prescribed to anyone. How did you get these?

BONNIE: The doctors were desperate, gave me all kinds of things to try to save her—

MOIRA: That's not how it works. They don't just hand over—

BONNIE: What do you know about it? You weren't there when they talked about treatments—specialist after specialist /sending me out with armfuls of, of medicines to try...

MOIRA: /These things don't even go together! Blood pressure medicines and, what is this? This powder here, /it's not even—

(BONNIE *snatches the bottle.*)

BONNIE: /Give that to me! I told you, they were always sending me home with new medicines—

MOIRA: THAT'S NOT HOW IT WORKS!

(MOIRA)

(*The bottles*)

MOIRA: That's not how it works...

(*The rabbits*)

MOIRA: Oh my god.

(*The shadows*)

MOIRA: What did you do?

BONNIE: I've had quite enough of all of this. I will not have you up here, raping memories, passing judgement on things you can't possibly understand—

(MOIRA *stares as* BONNIE *frantically stuffs the bottles and such back in their box.*)

MOIRA: And finally, something heavy starts to lift...

BONNIE: She was sick. I…I saved everything, in case she needed it again, you know? What's wrong with that? Pharmacies get expensive—

MOIRA: So you, what, created your own private pharmacy up here with stolen samples and potions?

BONNIE: —What stolen? I told you—

MOIRA: Up here with that cage full of…of/dead *pets*? Syringes and pills and lies…

BONNIE: /Goddammit Twigs, I can feel your eyes on the back of my head like acid, I can. Your venomous eyes… It's her medicines is all. I saved everything. Stop looking into me like that!

(The wind)

MOIRA: Everything is finally starting to— A snapping of something sincere and ancient in my marrow, even. Oh my god… Click.

BONNIE: What are you going on about?

MOIRA: A reckoning. That's what all this is. And daddy saw it—a poison…/*you're* Shiva. And after all this time you think you can unburden yourself of, of…some new kind of horror.// I've been…hiding from everything, in my own silent corner, but *you*, you—

BONNIE: /What's your father got to do with— // You're jumping to some mighty strong conclusions—

MOIRA: —Years wasted, my life *wasted*, pulverized by this mountain of…of…bullshit. Until… Click.

BONNIE: Will you quit it with that "Click" business?

(A CRACK of thunder and lightening as the house shakes.)

(The roof bends.)

MOIRA: *(Steel)* What happened to the rabbits?

BONNIE: What is your fascination with—

MOIRA: The rabbits, Mother, why are there so many pieces of them lying around?

BONNIE: Maeb wanted them.

MOIRA: These weren't pets.

BONNIE: They were a secret.

MOIRA: Why are they all dead?

BONNIE: Things die, Moira. I'm not a vet!

MOIRA: Did you kill them?

BONNIE: I think you hit your head harder than we thought—

MOIRA: Stop doing that, that redirection shit— You were practicing on them, weren't you? Like some kind of, of mad scientist?

BONNIE: You're not making sense—

MOIRA: You were practicing on *them*, so you'd know how much of that bullshit "medicine" you could get away with giving to Maeb…I always thought you were crazy…but you're—I mean, clinically speaking— you're really, really / sick.

BONNIE: /Twigs—

MOIRA: Was she ever really ill?

(MOIRA)

(*The universe*)

(*They tilt*)

(BONNIE *scrambles.*)

BONNIE: Stop being morbid! You heard the doctors, you know—

MOIRA: Was she ever really ill?

BONNIE: She was delicate.

MOIRA: She was innocent!

(*The house shakes.*)

MOIRA: Did she know? DID SHE KNOW WHAT YOU
WERE DOING TO HER?

BONNIE: How dare you accuse me of, of…I loved her!
You were the last one, Moira. Last one to see her! You
and your "hands". You said so yourself, guilt spread
crossed your face. Not five minutes ago, all pale and
ash-like right there.

MOIRA: Stop it!

BONNIE: You were the last one by her side, and so
worried about the bills. The money. Always trying to
escape, you were.

(BONNIE *and* MOIRA *move with the storm.*)

(*Rapid-fire*)

MOIRA: You don't know what you're talking about—

BONNIE: Wouldn't let me alone with her. Wouldn't
let anyone alone with her. Hovering over her with
your guilty conscious /to be sure, just plotting and
scheming—

MOIRA: /My guilty— Stop twisting…I won't let you do
this to me—

BONNIE: Scheming away how you were going to run
off with the farm once she'd done with us.

MOIRA: What? I loved her!

BONNIE: Oh, who's fooling who now, Moira Lane? You
always loved yourself first and best above the rest, isn't
that right? Not so different/ from me— She was newly
dead and barely cold before you were off to the races,
taking the bar—//

MOIRA: /You're changing the— //How dare you
insinuate I would hurt her for my own, my own gain!

BONNIE: What haunts you, Moira?/ Something dark, something heavy, something all yours.// You, you, you— What did you do?

MOIRA: /Nothing! //That body, it was ruined. She was never going to get out of that hospital, she was never going to get better, I could see it. *Everyone* could see—

BONNIE: Everyone was wrong! *I* knew she had more time. I KNEW WHAT SHE COULD TAKE!

(The air is gone.)

(Horror and rain)

(The roof bends and twists and is wrenched from it's roots.)

(MOIRA and her rage leap at BONNIE.)

(The pair topple down the ladder and land with a sickening THUMP.)

(The wind is wicked.)

(BONNIE and MOIRA scramble, trying to breathe, both returned [for the moment] to their primal beginnings.)

(They stare.)

(Neither blinks.)

(MOIRA contemplates her murderous hands…)

(Finally, language returns.)

MOIRA: …The world is flat—

BONNIE: No one ever tells you that children suck the life out of you. No one ever tells you that it won't be enough, no matter what you do—I loved ye both, but you needed so much from me. Practically sucked me dry— You were emotional little vampires. Always needing, always wanting *something* from me. I gave you life, wasn't that enough? Sucking the spirit out of me and I said NOTHING. I never put you out. I never let you go without. I was *dying for you!*

Then your sister came, uninvited… and there I was, loaning my body to another parasite, the air already gone… No one ever asked *me* how *I* felt about it!
I thought she'd be done with, the first time I—I thought for sure… And that would be the end of it, and they'd all of them know and send me away somewhere quiet… But everyone was so nice to us. So nice to *me*, and I got to sleep peaceful for the first time since she'd been born.
And she was fine, all the doctors and nurses to take care of her, fussing over her, she was just fine!
And she needed me, needed me to love her, to take care of her, I could do that for her because she was so weak, so fragile. She looked up at me with all that trust in her eyes, I was saving her. I was her savior.

MOIRA: Don't you dare use that word—

BONNIE: I'm telling you I never thought… never meant it to go the way that it did. Never ever never ever… But, this time since—the guilt? It's not all mine is it? This darkness is not all mine to carry, Moira?

MOIRA: Get away from me!

BONNIE: I hear your name.

MOIRA: I hate you!

BONNIE: There's bad tidings more on the wind! Something missing here amongst this mess, something keeping him from putting me out— Your name over and over and over again— Can't you hear it? MoiraMoiraMoiraLane…

MOIRA: I left…I left all of this…stop!

BONNIE: Those hands, Moira, please *tell me*!

MOIRA: I was so sure, so *sure*… Do you know how long I've felt this, darkness, this lingering anguish?

BONNIE: Moy—

MOIRA: I never *knew*. Never understood what was just under my nose. Heard, felt... maybe... But never thought...

BONNIE: MOIRA!

(MOIRA's hands)

MOIRA: This wind...

BONNIE: What did you do?

MOIRA: I saved her.

BONNIE: What do you mean? What do you mean, Twigs. /Tell us—

(The shadows converge.)

MOIRA: /I wept for you. *For you,* and for daddy... for all of us that would miss her. And I died with her when I—when I pressed that pillow to her face... Sure that it was right, but terrified—

(Thunder)

MOIRA: And all this time *I didn't know that you had already killed her!*

(BONNIE throws her arms wide to the wind and rain.)

BONNIE: From your tongue to his ears, pressed against my heart. *The truth shall set me free—*

MOIRA: You're not free of anything!

BONNIE: But you're the one, Twigs—*you're the one what done her in.* Not me after all, not me after all—

(MOIRA and her rage...)

(BONNIE and MOIRA collide.)

BONNIE: Two by two, me and you. No more magic, just us and dirt. And we to be buried in it by His hand, together!

MOIRA: STOP TALKING LIKE THERE'S SOMETHING SPECIAL HAPPENING HERE! YOU'RE NOT

SPECIAL! There's nobody here but me and you in the muck and mire —

BONNIE: And we're covered in it! Through and through... Our hands— The fruit fallen so close— Mother, daughter, mother, daughter, mother, daughter...

MOIRA: I *saved* her!

BONNIE: Oh, but that's the pickle isn't it? What I done or we done or you done or not done, it's all undone now. You and all this... Laid bare for Him to judge! So who's going to be saving you, Twigs?

(MOIRA, *lightning, the house*)

MOIRA: There's nothing left here to save... Just a puddle of me, and of mud!

(MOIRA'*s hands round* BONNIE'*s neck*)

(*Squeezing, wringing, pushing*)

(BONNIE *stumbles, her back pressed to the window...*)

(*The faery song on* BONNIE'*s lips as her body meets wall, and glass, then air...*)

MOIRA: (*As it happens*) Things tumbling around us, this damned ancient house full of cracks and lies, shivering, breaking, crackling white fire...reaching back into nothing but...wind and missed moments, and vapor...

(*The window*)

(*The window*)

(MOIRA *all alone.*)

(MOIRA *stares after her, hands shaking, breath gone from her.*)

(*The storm shudders.*)

MOIRA: ...and dust.

(*Silence*)

(Finally)

(Then…faintly…)

(A baby's cry on the wind.)

(MOIRA looks to the attic.)

MOIRA: What whispers this?

(The cries get louder.)

(MOIRA grabs a pillow, scrambling up the ladder…)

(There, the basket…she steps closer.)

(She and the pillow stare at Maeb…)

(Stare)

(Stare)

(She bends…)

(A cry drawn from the earth itself escapes her broken lips.)

(She puts down the pillow.)

(She picks up the "baby".)

(The wind caresses them both.)

MOIRA: Shh, shh, now. Everything's going to be alright.

(Black)

END OF PLAY

ADDENDUM

(Additional dialogue for BONNIE *and* WILLIAM *in ACT ONE Scene iii concerning the argument under* MOIRA*'s ascent to discovering Maeb:)*

BONNIE: Oh, here we go again… It's always about you, isn't it? What you did, what you earn, never accounting for all I do—

WILLIAM: Bah!

BONNIE: Always taking me for granted—Where do you think you're going?

WILLIAM: If you're going to be shouting at me all night, might as well be shouted at with a drink in my hand.

BONNIE: Rummy!

WILLIAM: Slut!

BONNIE: Oh, how I stayed married to you after all these years is beyond me— What was that?

WILLIAM: Don't know what you're squawking about, cant' hear nothing above you're shrill screaming.

BONNIE: Where's Moira? Moy? That fool girl…

A LIST OF MAYBES AND CHEAT CODES
for Directors, Designers, and Other Production Dreamers:
(or, "How the Heck Does Any of This Stuff Actually Happen?")

There are a multitude of ways one might go about bringing a house-shaking storm to life, and I'm excited about all of them! But because my stage directions might also feel a bit overwhelming, I've created a list of "Maybes" to help get you started. Please note, this list is not exhaustive, nor meant to be prescriptive! Rather, think of it as a jumping off point. And most of all, remember that your audience will eagerly suspend their disbelief. Nu Sass put this show up in an 18-seat studio space using sliding flats to delineate different rooms/floors, and they consistently freaked out/moved their audiences every night because they absolutely leaned in to making that small, intimate space the spookiest old house/fairy storm it could be. So, without further ado...

Maybe:

The house is a small-scale model suspended somewhere on stage, where it is inundated with mud/collapsed inward, while the rooms/action are staged in synch in full scale around it?

The house is just three floating (and minimally dressed) platforms that can collapse downward?

The house, and each of its crucial rooms, is all just projection?

The mud is made with lights and shadows?

The mud and moss are foam rubber chips and a dancer in a gilly suit (as done in the Nu Sass production)

The mud is actual mud and you do the play outside (maybe in an old cornfield) so that no one gets mad at you about the mud?

Cheat Codes:

Sound design for this play is key and can do a lot of the heavy lifting for you. In the Nu Sass production, the sound designer even included a wind-rendered whisper of the characters' names in some of ACT TWO named-beat moments, which was cool.

Have fun building Maeb. Make sure that Bonnie always holds her like a beloved infant, no matter how creepy her twigs and yarn body may be. Audiences will like to get a close look at her (maybe even a selfie?) after the show if you're willing.

In the Nu Sass production Willy's porcelain chips were the remains of a shattered white chocolate mug, which he picked up and put into a pre-set, non-shattered mug, which held a blood capsule inside. It was super effective.

Remember there is no "one way" to bring this play to life.

www.ingramcontent.com/pod-product-compliance
Lightning Source LLC
Chambersburg PA
CBHW052206090426
42741CB00010B/2424